Pocketbook of Prayers

PRAYERS FOR GROWING GIRLS

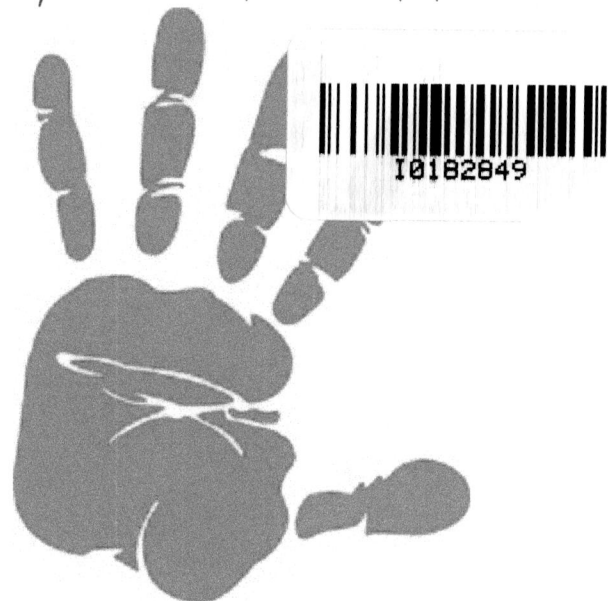

Monica L. Sanders, M.Div.

Copyright © 2016

Kingdom Living Publishing

All rights reserved. No part of this publication may be reproduced or transmitted in any form or by any means without permission of Kingdom Living Publishing Company. All Scriptures have been quoted from www.biblegateway.com, KJV, NIV, and MSG versions. All others cited directly. You may visit our website at www.stellarhall.com

ISBN-10:0-9888345-3-7

ISBN-13:978-0-9888345-3-8

This book is dedicated to my Grand-girls:

Janiyah Monica
11 years' old

Serenity Nevaeh
8 years' old

Kayla Elise
3 years old

Pray always!

Love you, Nanans

Matthew 6:9-13
New Revised Standard Version (NRSV)

9 "Pray then in this way:

Our Father in heaven,
hallowed be your name.
10   Your kingdom come.
Your will be done,
on earth as it is in heaven.
11   Give us this day our daily bread
12   And forgive us our debts,
as we also have forgiven
our debtors.
13   And do not bring us to the
time of trial,
but rescue us from the evil one.

PRAYERS

Parents
School
Friends
Siblings
Health
Behavior
Obedience
Death
Family Issues
Sick Pet
Love
Good Morning
Good Night

for Parents

Dear Lord,
We are grateful for our parents.
We are blessed to have parents that love us.
We are thankful that you allow them to provide for me.
We ask that you continue to keep them healthy.
Continue to keep them safe.
Continue to give them direction for our lives as we grow.
In Jesus Name, AMEN!

Pray
for School

God,

As the school year approaches,

I am scared and nervous.

I want to make the right decisions.

I want to have true friends.

I want favor with my teachers.

Let my thoughts be focused on my work and what I should achieve.

I ask this in Jesus Name, AMEN!

for Friends

My heavenly friend,
Friendship is important to me.
I value the relationships that you have given me.
I ask to have the true bond and alliances that honor you.
I ask you to grant me acquaintances that I can grow with.
I desire friends that are both honest and long lasting.
In Jesus precious name, AMEN!

for Siblings

Dear Sweet Jesus,
Thank you for allowing me sibling(s).
Thank you for our relationship.
Thank you for making us friends.
Please keep my sibling(s) (name) from all danger.
Please keep my sibling(s) out of harm's way of the devil.
Please allow their lives to shine bright for others to see.
Allow me to be a blessing to them especially by listening and loving them.
Allow me to help my sibling(s) with their dreams and visions.
I ask this in Jesus' name and seal it,
AMEN!

for
Good Health

Dear Great God,
You tell us that our body is a temple.
Help us to keep our body strong.
Help us to understand how to eat right.
Help us to exercise and be fit.

Help us to learn and teach how important it is to exercise.
Help us to be healthy in not only our body, but our mind.
Help us to understand our physical condition is important to you and for others.
We ask these things in Jesus' name.
AMEN!

for Behavior

Almighty GOD,

We come to Thank you

for all you have done.

We ask you to help us to conduct

ourselves so that you will be happy.

We ask you to show us the way to be

more like you in our actions.

We ask you to direct our attitude.

We ask you to direct our manners.

We ask you to direct our ways.

We ask for your help in every deed by

word and action.

In Jesus' name, AMEN!

for Obedience

God,
Please help me respect others.
Help me to regard your ways.
Help me to show esteem to those
you have placed over me.
Help me to honor good character.
Help me to hold dear what is right
and disallow what is wrong.
Help me to admire those who obey
and follow their paths.
Help me to submit to authority that
is in your authority.
I pray this in Jesus' name that it will
be done. AMEN!

for the Passing of a Loved One

Dear God,

Today I lost my friend.

They say she passed away.

I'm not sure what that mean, but I know she is gone.

I feel that my heart is broken.

Can you come by and fix it?

I am not sure about this feeling, but

I know I don't want it

Thank you God, AMEN!

 for
Family Issues

Jesus, My Mommy and Daddy are
not doing fine.
They yell and scream and tell me it's
nothing.
I'm calling you up to come and see
about my family,
Because I love them.
And don't want them to yell and
scream anymore at each other.
In your name I pray,
AMEN!

for Sick Pet

Oh God,

My pet has not been doing well.

We took him to the doctor today.

They said he is very sick.

Lord what should we do?

I love him so much.

God, can you help?

AMEN!

for Love

Jesus,
Thank you for your love.
Thank you for your care.
Thank you that you make all things better.
Knowing you are here,
helps me feel safe.
Knowing you love me, make me feel happy.
Thank you God for Jesus.
AMEN!

for a Good Morning

Dear God
Thank you for waking me up this morning.
Thank you for keeping me through the night.
Guide me as I tackle the things
that I must go through
on this day.
Thank you for loving me
AMEN!

for A Good Night

Dear God,
It's been a long day.
I hope I passed my spelling test.
I hope I was a good friend,
but most of all I pray
that you keep me
until tomorrow to make a difference.
Give us sweet rest and peace
through the night.
Protect us as we sleep.
Wake us up to love, care and be
what you want us to be.
AMEN!

Take time to write your own prayer to ask God to help you with what you need help with
SUBJECT:

_____
_____
_____
_____
_____
_____
_____
_____
_____
_____
_____
_____
_____
_____
_____
_____
_____
_____

Take time to write your own prayer to ask God to help you with what you need help with

SUBJECT:

_____
_____
_____
_____
_____
_____
_____
_____
_____
_____
_____
_____
_____
_____
_____
_____
_____

Special Thanks and Love to all those who pray especially for our children.

We continue to trust God for their success in Kingdom Living as they form their relationship with God through prayer.

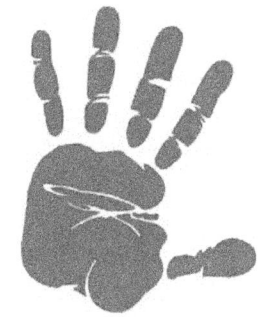

Monica L. Sanders

ABOUT THE AUTHOR

Monica L. *Sanders* *is a Senior Pastor, Author, and Prayer Warrior. A native of Washington, DC she is a mother of three young adult children and four grandchildren. Pastor Sanders has been married to Fredricks L. Sanders, Sr. for 25 years and they reside in Charlotte, North Carolina.*

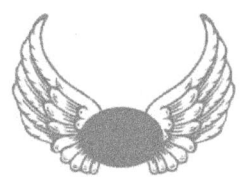